Pawleys Island
PARADISE

*To Jill —
One of my
favorite readers!*

Pawleys Island PARADISE
A COMPANION

Laurie Larsen

LAURIE LARSEN

RANDOM MOON BOOKS
A PHASE FOR EVERY FANCY

Pawleys Island Paradise: A Companion
Copyright © 2016 by Laurie Larsen
Published by Random Moon Books

All rights reserved. No part of this book may be used or reproduced in any manner whatsoever without written permission of the author except in the case of brief quotations embodied in critical articles or reviews.

All Content by author Laurie Larsen
All photographs taken by Laurie Larsen
Cover Art by Steven Novak
Formatting by Go Published

Print ISBN -13: 978-1533375773
Print ISBN-10: 1533375771
Ebook ISBN: 978-0-9975630-0-9

Published in the United States of America

A breezy spring day on Pawleys Island. To get the shot we had to curve around the bend, park the car illegally and run back in the wind to get it. My husband begrudgingly agreed. ☺

TABLE OF CONTENTS

In the Beginning 1
How Pawleys Island Paradise Was Born 7
Fact or Fiction? 13
The Brookgreen Stallions 17
The Old Gray Barn 21
The Seaside Inn 25

IN THE BEGINNING

Growing up, it was a family priority to go on vacation every year. My dad was a corporate businessman and my mom was a first grade teacher, so our vacations always occurred in the summer. I learned early on from my parents that the only decent summer vacation was to THE BEACH! My parents loved the beach, and therefore, I love the beach. I don't remember going on a family vacation that didn't involve the beach. I immediately associated the sound of the waves, the taste of the salt, the feel of the sand in my bare toes, as some of the most wonderful and freeing feelings in the world.

Because I grew up in central Illinois, it took a LONG TIME to get to the beach. During my childhood, we tried a lot of beaches. One time we took a 4-day car trip out west to San Francisco where we visited the beautifully chilly and rocky Pacific Ocean. One year we drove south and booked a condo for a week at beautiful New Smyrna Beach, Florida. We were having such a great time that we ended up extending our trip spontaneously and staying an extra week.

But once we discovered Pawleys Island, South Carolina, we were hooked and ended up going back there time and time again. I grew up in a family that, until late in my high school years, we were isolated (geographically) from other family members. In other words, I didn't have grandparents, aunts, uncles or cousins in the same town as me. In order to see family, we had to travel. And we did. We traveled to Ohio, Tennessee, California and Massachusetts to visit family members and stay in their houses. But the best solution was for all family members to travel to the beach and get a house to stay in together, and spend a week or two or three, vacationing.

I don't remember how, but we somehow discovered The Old Gray Barn in Pawleys Island. Cousins from all over the country went there and we spent the vacation re-connecting while playing in the sand, swimming in the ocean, nursing our sunburns, and playing endlessly. And every year, we went back.

The Old Gray Barn met our needs. It was big, slept a ton of people, and sat right on the beach. No outside entertainment was needed during the day. All the kids would just wake up, eat breakfast and head out the back door and entertain themselves for hours at a time with the sand and surf.

It has not escaped me how "unluxurious" these vacations were, especially compared to the beach vacations we take now. Like my parents did, my husband and I take our own family on a beach vacation every year. But unlike my parents, we usually book a 2-bedroom condo with air conditioning, two baths, a fully stocked kitchen and a flat screen TV! Not only is it beachfront, but there's also a pool at our disposal, as well as usually an exercise room and hot tubs. We don't cook big family meals every night like we did in the old days. We stock cereal and sandwich stuff to make our own breakfasts and lunches, and then we hit the town to find the ultimate seafood restaurants for dinner. I admire my mom and my aunts who worked so hard during these vacations of my childhood, to make sure that everyone was having a good time, while not spending a mint.

Oh, and did I mention that while driving across the country from the Midwest to the beach, my family would camp at campgrounds at night? My parents would pack our station wagon with a tent, sleeping bags, cooking utensils, etc., for nights spent camping. Yowza. My family now? We check into the closest Hampton Inn!

When I was putting together my exclusive "Pawleys Island: Then and Now" photo album for my Book 1 – 3 boxset, I went over to my parents' house and dug through boxes and photo albums until I found what I was looking for. Here are some of the treasures I unearthed:

The Old Gray Barn circa 1965 from the back

This isn't the whole group that stayed in The Old Gray Barn but it's close. I believe all we're missing is my grandpa, who was most likely taking the photo.

Me with my grandpa and my cousin, David.

One memorable afternoon, we went fishing at the pier of the house of some friends, in 1971. My cousin Cindy caught a huge snapping turtle on her crab line.

My brother Chris and my cousin Scott with the fruits of their labor.

Cousins digging in the sand, just like Stella (Tom and Marianne's daughter) loves to. I'm the blonde one in the front, turning around. I always loved that "bubble" bathing suit.

How Pawleys Island Paradise Was Born

It was in the early summer of 2011. I had been a published author for eleven years, but I was struggling with where my writing career was going. I'd been published by three separate publishing companies, and although each one had been an improvement over the last, I had never managed to achieve the kind of readership that would make me a successful writer. I had written eight books, and within those books I had written several different genres: contemporary romance, women's fiction/family saga and Young Adult romance. I was trying to find my niche, a place where my writing style – my voice – was a natural fit. I had dabbled with independent publishing with my last couple books, and I was learning a lot, but I had a long way to go to be considered successful.

I wrote standalone books, and although they are good reads, for the most part, well-written, it was very difficult to produce something that would stand out. I was a needle in a haystack. If someone found my books, they usually enjoyed them. And occasionally they sought out more.

One thing I knew: I didn't want to quit writing all together. Writing was such a huge part of my life that I couldn't imagine life without it. BUT (and this was a big but …) I didn't see the point in just going down the same path I'd been on. Write another entertaining, but easily forgettable contemporary romance novel. I desperately needed to make a change for the better.

Meanwhile, as I learned more and more about indie publishing, I was hearing that connected books in a series were popular. E-book readers who loved Book 1 of a series could easily download Book 2 and keep reading.

I also learned that releasing books in much closer succession made it easier to be successful with indie publishing. When published by a publishing house, you were lucky to get one book out every 12 to 18 months. But indie authors can literally hit publish as often as they had quality material ready.

So I had three problems to overcome:

1. I was growing tired of contemporary romance and the "forget-ability" of my stories.

2. I needed to think of a series to offer.

3. I needed to write and publish more books, more often.

So I started brainstorming. What did I want to create?

1. Something meaningful. Heartwarming. Inspiring.

2. A story that makes people feel good.

3. A story that will be remembered long after it is finished.

A few weeks of letting my brain mull this over, and I had the beginning premise of a story. I went to the baseball game of my younger son and I said to Anne, a fellow-mom, and also an avid reader. "What do you think of this as a story?

Would you want to read something like this?" I pitched the story of a woman in her 50's who thought that life was all set – long-term marriage, successful career, ambitious daughter – only to discover that her whole life was falling apart. Her husband strayed, her marriage is ending, her school year is coming to an end, and her daughter accepted an internship out of the country. All that spread out in front of her was a long, empty, lonely summer. So, she decides to hit the road. Have no destination in mind, just follow the path where God leads her and she discovers that as broken and devastated as we are, God can use our unique skillset to help others that He puts in our path. After following God's will, the woman realizes that what started out to be the worst summer of her life, turns into one of the best.

    The pitch just flowed off my tongue. Anne stared at me, spellbound as I blabbered the entire premise. And when I stopped she said, "YES! Yes, I'd love to read that. That's me. That's you. That's every woman our age. Maybe the details aren't the same for everyone, but the thought that God can use us, flaws and all, makes it very universal and appealing."

    So, a budding excitement in my heart, I took the idea and expanded on it a little more. Leslie Malone was born, as was her ex-husband Tim, her daughter Jasmine, all the characters she met along the way, and of course, eventually, Hank Harrison and the whole Harrison gang.

    I needed a place where her roadtrip would end – an ultimate destination. I needed to think of a place that could be home base for Leslie this summer, somewhere I knew, somewhere I loved.

    Ding ding ding! Of course. It had to be Pawleys Island!

    Once I'd gotten that far, I prayed. It really felt like I was going to be writing an inspirational romance. Not a total genre shift for me. I had written an inspirational romance before, my 2009 book *Preacher Man*, which earned me some international accolades when it won the prestigious EPIC Award for Best Spiritual Romance of 2010. I felt like I could build on that.

But I couldn't do it without some help and guidance from my Father. I prayed about this story. I prayed about my writing career. I felt like I was on the verge of something big, and God placed some excitement in my heart. I made a deal with God (smile). I told Him that if He wanted me writing Christian fiction, He needed to guide the right readers to me. I had spent eleven years becoming the best writer I knew how to be. I'd sharpened my shovel, I'd practiced and perfected my trade. Now, I would be writing for Him. He just needed to put the books in front of those people who needed/wanted to hear the message.

So, we settled on an agreement. Every day when I sat down to write, I prayed, "God, guide this story. Guide my words. Help me to write the story that You want me to tell. And help this book, and all my others, find the readers. Amen."

Five finished books later, I still pray that prayer every day.

Did it work? Yes. I have no doubt that God wants me writing this series about this group of people learning life's lessons that others can learn from them. Book 1 was released in 2014 to a modest debut. But once Book 2 was released, I went back and made the e-book of Book 1 FREE. It's called a Loss Leader. Take a loss on Book 1 with the hope that enough readers will love it and seek out Book 2.

With Book 1 free for over a year now, the book has been downloaded by over 150,000 readers. It currently has over 350 reviews with an average of 4.6 stars out of 5. Best of all, I've gotten so many reviews and personal messages telling me how important that book is to them. How meaningful it is for them, how it's helped them through the pain of divorce. It has reached way more people than any of my other books, and I believe it happened because of that deal I made with God.

Books 2, 3 and 4 all released to excellent sales as well. Book 2 was a #1 Amazon bestseller, and my 3-book boxset was a #1 Amazon bestseller for a week straight. I don't relay this to brag. I'm merely showing that God was true to His word. This was meaningful fiction that reached a lot of people, memorable after the last page was read.

God took care of my other two problems too: when I was halfway through writing *Roadtrip to Redemption*, I realized that I'd introduced quite a lot of characters. Leslie's daughter, Hank's son, Hank's daughter and granddaughter. Could I dream up stories featuring each of these people and hook them together as a series? Why, yes. Yes, I could.

And that resolved my third problem: writing faster. I'd always been the type of writer to write one book a year. But suddenly, I was writing faster. I didn't have to end one book, and dream up a whole new plot, all new characters. I knew these people. They were inside me. The books pick up where the last one stopped, so I am in a flow. And the previous book hints at what the next feature couple's conflict is – the beginning of the next story.

So far, I've been writing and releasing two books a year. Not a landspeed record, but definitely an amazing accomplishment for me.

Now, I'm one book away from finishing this wonderful and blessed series. I'll miss them. I'll miss these families desperately! I don't want to leave Pawleys Island! I don't want to leave the Harrisons. But I have to. I can't really imagine any stories following Book 6. And I want to end the series as it started: on a strong note. Inspiring. Uplifting. Heartwarming. I can only hope that God will reveal the next big idea when it's time.

Fact or Fiction?

When writing about a place I love as much as Pawleys Island, a place where I've spent a lot of time, I can't help but incorporate my own personal experiences into the storyline, experienced by characters within the novel.

For example, in Book 1 Leslie tells Hank the story about how when she was a kid, she and her cousin Margaret (with lovely dark brown hair) went out into the waves on an inflatable raft, and experienced a terribly painful episode. Later they discovered that Leslie's leg had been captured by a Portguese Man O' War. Leslie's mother created a poultice of herbs, wrapped her leg, made Leslie stay inside for the next couple of days. To make her feel better, Leslie's mother took her to the library in town and let her pick out a whole stack of horse books.

ALL OF THAT happened to me! Word for word. In fact, here's a peek at me and my cousin Margaret, quite possibly the very summer that it happened:

Part of the gang – I'm the blonde in the striped shorts, second from the left in the front. Standing to the left is my cousin Margaret, of the Portuguese Man o' War story fame, featured in Roadtrip to Redemption.

In Book 2, Jeremy is dating Emma. I needed a local restaurant for him to take her to. I did some internet research and found a list of restaurants to choose from. One jumped out at me: Quigley's Pint and Pub. One of my best friends, and a bridesmaid in my wedding is Kathy Quigley. So I chose that one. I only mentioned it in one brief scene, but she recognized it and made a point to thank me for picking it. Recently we were visiting Pawleys and I posed in front of the restaurant and sent her this pic:

The Brookgreen Stallions

My dad's little sister's name was Nancy. She was an artist, a painter. It seemed extremely artistic and bohemian to me when she changed the spelling of her own name to Nan-c. Aunt Nan-c taught me how to draw horses one summer in the Old Gray Barn. She sat with the patience of a saint and gave me techniques for drawing the head, the mane, the legs, the body and the tail. By the end of the vacation, I was very pleased with my ability to draw a pretty realistic-looking horse.

Near Pawleys Island is a beautiful attraction called Brookgreen Gardens. The driveway into the place features a stunning silver statue of two stallions fighting. I'd never seen anything like it. Neither, evidently, had Aunt Nan-c. One summer day, she took her sketch pad, drove over to Brookgreen Gardens, sat on a folding chair and drew for hours. Later, that sketch became her next painting project. Imagine the awe of a little horse-crazy girl, who Aunt Nan-c had spent time teaching how to sketch horses, when she came home with a real, grown-up artist's rendering of fighting stallions.

I'm thrilled to report that Aunt Nan-c's treasured horse painting has now found a resting place in my house!

*Aunt Nan-c's inspiration (above)
and her final creation (below)*

The Old Gray Barn

When I was writing *Roadtrip to Redemption,* my family took our annual beach vacation. This year we happened to go to Myrtle Beach, SC. One day we were driving around and I saw a sign for Pawleys Island. I hadn't been there in decades, but I immediately wanted to try to find the old house where my family spent summer after summer. The only problem was, I had no idea where it was. I didn't have an address, and it had been so long since I'd been to the area, that I had no clear memory of how the island was even configured. But how hard could it be? I knew it was an older home, and I knew the back faced the ocean. I knew it was on a small dirt road, and a saltwater marsh faced the front, with a fishing pier.

At least that's how it looked back in the 1960s!

So we headed to the ocean. My husband was driving and I had my eyes peeled, waiting for some type of memory to hit. I realized that I might have a better chance of recognizing it if I saw it from the back, so I jumped out of the car and told my husband to keep in touch by cellphone. He'd drive the roads looking at the fronts of the houses; I'd walk the beach and look at the backs of the houses.

A shady plan, at best. But then a miracle happened. My cell phone rang and my husband said, "I think I found it. It's called The Old Gray Barn, right?" I squealed and affirmed. I walked back to the street, and he swung around to pick me up.

The minute I saw it, I felt like I'd gone home again. We were meant to find that old wooden house on stilts. It held so many wonderful memories.

The Old Gray Barn circa 2011. I snapped this pic, which was featured on the cover of *Roadtrip to Redemption*. The driveway is made of a "seashell mulch." I used to sit with a colander and strain the tiny conch shells through, just like Stella did in *Journey to Fulfillment*.

How I knew I'd found it when we were wandering around, looking for the house.

We parked in the driveway and I bravely walked up the big wooden front porch, and knocked on the door. A cleaning crew was inside, getting the house ready for its next set of renters. They graciously allowed me to come inside and look all around. The rooms looked similar, but more modern. For example, the house had been upgraded with central air conditioning, something we never had when I used to vacation there. And there was a big, flat-screen TV. I don't remember there being any TV at all!

Hanging on the wall in the living room were framed photos of the Old Gray Barn in the throes of Hurricane Hugo in 1989. The houses on either side of the Barn were completely demolished. But the Barn withstood with little or no damage. I shuddered to think that just like that, the house containing all my memories could have been thrown out to sea. But it survived.

When I wrote the scene of Leslie arriving at The Old Gray Barn after her long roadtrip, I pulled on that experience directly. Of course, instead of encountering a cleaning crew, she encountered a certain tall, rugged and handsome handyman fixing some boards on the back porch.

Well, there had to be a romance!! And so the romance of Leslie and Hank begins ...

The back porch of The Old Gray Barn – a perfect place to rock and relax, like so many of the Harrison characters do.

The view from the back porch

The Seaside Inn

When I was writing Roadtrip (Book 1), I knew I wanted Hank's daughter Marianne and her husband Tom to own and operate a beachfront inn. I had a pretty specific idea in my mind what it would look like, but I'd never actually been to one like it. So I hit the internet, and did searches on oceanfront inns in Pawleys Island. There are several, but I landed on one that hit the mark. The website showed many photos of the front, the back, and the cute and cozy guest rooms. Based on that website, I created Marianne's Seaside Inn.

The actual inn that inspired the Seaside Inn is called the Sea View Inn. I contacted the inn and asked if they would mind if I called the inn by name in my book. They suggested that I change it slightly, thus the Seaside Inn was born.

Recently, my husband and I visited the Sea View Inn so I could see my inspiration in real life. It's charming and rustic, although not at all like the place that has now been featured prominently in all five of the books of the series. It's taken on a life of its own. Here are a few shots from that recent visit.

The Sea View Inn from the back (oceanfront).

I hope for those of you who have enjoyed the Pawleys Island Paradise series, that you've also enjoyed this companion book of behind the scenes stories. So what's next? Book 6 will be the finale of the series, and will tie up all the loose ends of all the characters' storylines. At this time, I plan to make Rita and Gary the feature couple. Do you remember Rita from Book 1? She owned the restaurant in her home called the Front Porch, and she was having trouble with her son Nathan. Leslie was able to help her out by giving her a mother's eye view on what Rita was doing to inadvertently make Nathan unable to stand on his own two feet.

After that, I'll offer a 6-book boxset available for download, and *then* I'm thinking of producing the books for Audio, with myself as the narrator! I've never done anything like that before but I think it would be fun!

In closing, I want to thank you, thank you, *thank you* for your loving support of these special characters and books. It really has been a huge pleasure to write them, and I can't tell you how much I appreciate you reading them.

Life's a beach,
Laurie

A Tribute

Every author has a favorite author. Someone whose writing speaks to them, someone they aspire to and learn from. Mine is Pat Conroy. Pat passed away recently and it caused me to write this tribute to him.

March 4, 2016
This morning I discovered that my favorite author in the world, Pat Conroy passed away. He'd been fighting pancreatic cancer for just a few weeks. He went quickly.

Pat's books had a strong effect on me, more than any other author I'd ever encountered. They made my heart sing, they made me cry. His sentences made me marvel that an author can create and craft thoughts in such a perfect way to create a response in their readers. I can only dream of reaching readers at a fraction of the way his books have touched me.

I never had the pleasure of meeting Pat in person, but I felt like I knew him because his writings, both fiction and non-fiction were so deeply personal, he invited his millions of readers into his life, pulling up a chair for us all at the table. Once, when I'd received a particularly brutal critique from a fellow writer, ripping my current manuscript apart, I went into a writing "depression," lost all my confidence and couldn't write for four months. Instead, I went back to Pat's books and read each of them, one by one, in order. Eventually, they healed my writing soul. They raised my spirits and made me whole again.

Not knowing if he would ever see it, I found an email address for Pat on the internet and sent him a heart-felt note, describing this whole experience, thanking him for helping me find my writer's voice again. To my absolute delight, I got a personal note back from him the very next day! Pat was, famously, not a typist, and I could tell from his response. He used punctuation, but no capital letters. He apologized for his awful typing, explaining that the son of a Marine fighter pilot was not allowed to take typing in school. Then he went on to commiserate with me about my writing crisis, and said that the creation of each of his books had caused him to sink into a deep depression while he was writing them, and he ended by saying he was glad that I'd weathered my tsunami.

It meant so much to me that he related to my pains, and responded personally to me. I will never forget it.

Once, a week before his book, *South of Broad* was released, my family was vacationing in Charleston. We stayed in an historic bed and breakfast in the South of Broad. Knowing Pat's history as well as I did, and knowing that his alma mater was The Citadel in Charleston, we took an excursion there and walked around the campus. Much of it was familiar to me from reading *The Lords of Discipline*. Only weeks later, after his new novel was released (which I devoured, by the way) and he wrote a blog post on his website, did I realize that Pat and his agent and his editor were also on The Citadel campus, that same day!! He wanted to give them a personal tour of the school that had meant so much to him and his growing years as an author. We didn't run into them, but we could've, and somehow in my mind, these two experiences bond us, connect us.

So, on this sad day of his passing, I want to thank Pat for the many hours of entertainment reading his novels, for the education his books have given me as a writer and especially for reaching out personally with his encouragement. I'll miss your future books, but I'm appreciative that you've left us with hours and hours of re-reads.

— Laurie

Gorgeous Pawleys Island, SC – life's a beach!

OTHER CHRISTIAN FICTION NOVELS BY LAURIE LARSEN

THE PAWLEYS ISLAND PARADISE SERIES:

Book 1: Roadtrip to Redemption. *It started as a trip to lose old memories. It became a journey to find her heart.* A woman facing the most desolate summer of her life, follows God's direction and instead has the most rewarding and life-changing summer of all.

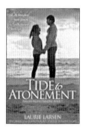

Book 2: Tide to Atonement. *Life knocked him down. Faith raised him up.* A man has paid his debt to society and is released from prison. Determined to create a life to be proud of, he realizes his past isn't quite as willing to be done as he wants it to be.

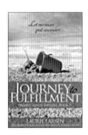

Book 3: Journey to Fulfillment. *A traumatic family event. Distinctly opposite ways of dealing with it between husband and wife. Let no man put asunder.* A married couple deals with a family tragedy in different ways and works through the resulting collapse of their marriage to reconcile their love for each other.

Book 4: Bridge to Fruition. *The old is gone. The new is come.* A young woman from an affluent family finds love with a man who grew up in the foster system. Can they let go of the trappings of their past and find love together in their present?

Book 5: Path to Discovery. Brokenhearted, New York actress Roxanne Frazier welcomes the escape from the hustle and bustle of the big city to take the lead in a beach-town dinner theater show. But then he walks in...Back into her life. And her memories of her worst nightmare.

Pawleys Island Paradise boxset: First three books in one easy download!

Laurie's 2010 EPIC Award winner for Best Spiritual Romance of 2010: **Preacher Man.** A beautiful, heartwarming Christian love story that will leave you feeling good.

WANT TO STAY IN TOUCH WITH LAURIE?

Her website/blog
authorlaurielarsen.com/

Her Facebook
www.facebook.com/authorlaurielarsen

Her Twitter
twitter.com/AuthorLaurie

Her Goodreads
www.goodreads.com/author/show/412692.Laurie_Larsen

Sign up to be on her newsletter mailing list: *authorlaurielarsen.com/newsletter-signup*. You'll get advance notice of all reviews, chances to win prizes and receive free giveaways!

Made in the USA
Charleston, SC
01 June 2016